1

Magnificent Obsession

Cultivating a Passion for the Passion of God

by Josh Hunt

Also by Josh Hunt

Books
You Can Double Your Class in Two Years or Less
Disciplemaking Teachers (with Dr. Larry Mays)
Enjoying God
Double Services; Double Sunday Schools
You Can Double Your Church in Five Years or Less
One Magnificent Obsession

Videos:
Family Life
One Solitary Life
Five Prayers
This Book Can Change Your Life
God We Enjoy
Enjoying God
T.I.G.E.R. Training: Eight Things Teachers Must Have From Their Staff to Double
You Can Double Your Church in Five Years or Less
The F.A.C.T.S. About Doubling Classes
Promises! Promises!
Disciplemaking Teachers
You Can Double Your Class in Two Years or Less

Copyright © 2003 Josh Hunt
All rights reserved
Josh Hunt
Las Cruces, NM 88011
505 532 9693
josh@joshhunt.com
www.joshhunt.com

ISBN: 0-9710675-4-6

Note: all scripture quotations are from NIV unless otherwise noted.

Verses marked NLT are from the New Living Translation
Verses marked LIVING are from the Living Bible

Commendations

Josh Hunt has done a tremendous job in setting forth a challenge of growing and reaching out through Bible Study groups. The dream to double at stated intervals is a worthy goal and one that is obtainable. He has given "how to" in a very clear and straightforward way. I commend this book to all who want to see their Bible Study grow.

Jimmy Draper
Lifeway Christian Resources

Josh Hunt has a passion for the lost and the hurting. Even more importantly, Jesus has a passion for the lost and hurting. *One Magnificent Obsession* is not a book about numbers and statistics. It is about a passion to reach and help the people behind the numbers. Read this book and be prepared to have your heart change to see God's Kingdom grow.

Thom Rainer
Dean, The Billy Graham School
Southern Baptist Theological Seminary

Josh is onto something in this book. The challenge of doubling in two years is more a matter of will than of knowing how. This book will help any leader cultivate a heart for what I see surfacing among most of the emerging churches–a heart for multiplication.

Bill Easum
President, Easum, Bandy & Associates
www.easumbandy.com

Josh Hunt is the master of practicality. If you want to know how it works, ask Josh Hunt.

Aubrey Malphurs

One Magnificent Obsession
Table of Contents

One Magnificent Obsession

John Piper quotes a Readers's Digest article[1] that reads:

> Bob and Penny took early retirement from their jobs in the northeast five years ago. She was 59 and he was 51. Now they live in Punta Gorda, Florida, where they cruise on their 30-foot trawler, play softball, and collect shells.

Bob and Penny are living the American dream: get a good job, make some money, retire early, move to Florida, and spend the remaining years of your life leisurely strolling on the beach. Drift on your boat, play softball, and collect seashells. It is the American Dream.

The plan for doubling is simple: give the ministry to laymen who are using their gifts to grow their groups to double their classes every two years or less.

There are people spending millions trying to get you to buy this dream. I invite you to a different life-mission. I invite you to one magnificent obsession: be the church that doubles. My dream is to see the Church double in the next 20 years. I want it to be your dream too.

Jesus left us some pretty simple instructions as he left. "Go, make disciples of everyone." Doubling groups is an expression of

---

[1]John Piper, "Boast Only In the Cross," *Passion*, One Day Live, DVD, perf. various artists, Sparrow/Emd, 2000.

obedience to that command. In fact, whether your church is into the "seeker" model or hates the "seeker" model, you have to have doubling groups in order to grow. If your church grows through a T.V. ministry, servant evangelism, visitation, or revivals, you have to have doubling groups to have a doubling church. All growing churches have one thing in common: they have doubling groups. It is Great Commission Fulfillment 101.

This is what I call the Iron Law of group life. You double a church by doubling the number of groups, not by doubling the size of each group. Every church fulfilling the Great Commission does so through doubling groups.

As I speak at conferences, promoting this dream, I often ask my host when he takes me back to the airport: "What advice do you have for me in helping the Church to double?" One host wisely responded: "I think you are going to need a lot of help." He is right. I need your help. I am asking you to give your life to the magnificent obsession of seeing the Church double in the next 20 years. Won't you join me in dreaming, praying, and helping?

The plan for doubling is simple: give the ministry to laymen who are using their gifts to grow their groups to double their classes every two years or less. By "groups" we mean any kind of group–Sunday School class, home Bible Study, and so forth.

In my previous book, *You Can Double Your Class in Two Years or Less,* I describe a five-part plan for doubling a group every two years or less. We will briefly overview that plan later. However, in my experience, the key issue is not so much the execution of the plan as it is the passion with which the plan is executed. You already know how to double a group. Let me illustrate.

Imagine that you attended an average sized group this past Sunday morning. Imagine that there were 15 adults in attendance in your Sunday School class. Suppose I could offer you a million dollars on the fourth consecutive Sunday that you had more than 30 people there. How long would it take you to double your group?

Imagine that something horrible would happen if you didn't double your group. Imagine that you would lose your own health or the life of your child if you didn't double within two years. Don't you think you could figure out how to double your group if the motivation was high enough?

In this volume I would like to give you 12 reasons to give your one and only life to the magnificent obsession of seeing the worldwide Church double in the next 20 years. The work is enjoyable and eternal in significance. Will you help?

Reason #1: The Joy of the Work

I think group work is more fun than Six Flags. The happiest people I know are leaders of groups that are doubling every two years or less. If you didn't have any high, holy, glorious, noble ambition in your life but just to have fun, I would invite you to give your life to doubling your group every two years or less. It is fun stuff.

Christian Swartz has done one of the most exhaustive studies ever conducted on the worldwide Church. He originally surveyed people on every continent in more than 1,000 churches, amassing 4.2 million bits of data. One of his findings: growing churches laugh more than non-growing churches.

> **Growing churches laugh more than non-growing churches.**

They are having more fun. Yes, we do have serious, heady, heavy reasons for giving our one and only lives to doubling. But I want to say right up front that this is a wonderful way to live.

There is a cost involved, a great cost. Our Master asked that we give up everything to be His followers (Luke 14:33). But the cost is richly rewarded. We are never asked to give up more than we get back. We give our rags to put on His royalty. It is worth it.

There will be some disappointment along the way. You will be hurt, rejected, and disappointed. People will not always respond to your love. They will reject you. I teach a very personal ministry, and when people reject you, it hurts. We are rejected as Christ was rejected. We share in his sufferings. [2]

Meet my friend Chris Thixton. Chris loves life. You can see it in his vibrant, expressive face. Chris is having fun doubling his class. He lives in Ozark, Missouri. I have been to his church twice. He has doubled his group numerous times. His method is not "Giving Friday Nights to Jesus" as I discuss in *You Can Double Your Class in Two Years or Less.* Instead he uses pizza on Sunday.

He roams the auditorium before the 11:00 service. Finding newcomers, he stops and introduces himself, engaging them in a friendly conversation. Soon, he pitches the bait: you guys like pizza? He directs the question at the kids, then turns to the parents to explain: "A bunch of us are going to get pizza after a while. If you want, I'd love for ya'll to come with us. I'd love to buy your pizza." He grew his class from 4 to 40 in 9 months using this method. (By the way, would you spend $25 a week to double your class? I told you it might cost you.)

> **We are happiest, not when we are in greatest comfort; rather, we are happiest when we are lost in a great cause.**

---

[2] "Now if we are children, then we are heirs–heirs of God and co-heirs with Christ, if indeed we share in his sufferings in order that we may also share in his glory" (Romans 8:17).

I cannot emphasize enough that Chris is exceptionally happy. He is one of the happiest church members I know. He is happy, in part, because he is engaged in the pursuit of a great cause. He has embraced the magnificent obsession. Just as in the parable of the talents, Chris is seeking to be the servant who takes what he has been given and doubles it.

Happiness is not so much about prosperity, ease, and creature comforts as it is about losing ourselves in a great cause. We are happiest, not when we are in greatest comfort; rather, we are happiest when we are lost in a great cause. The happiest people I know are lost in a magnificent obsession.

Do you want to be happy? I invite you to lose yourself in the magnificent obsession of using your gifts to help your group double every two years or less.

John Piper points out something interesting about happiness. The world teaches us that in order to be happy we need to have high self-esteem. We need to feel good about ourselves. We need to feel big. This is not the whole story.

> **We are happiest when we feel small standing before something great.**

Imagine a group of people leaning over the railing at the Grand Canyon, drinking in the view. They are lost in amazement and wonder. You stand beside them and casually remark, "Doesn't the Canyon make you feel good about yourself? Doesn't it make you feel big?"

"What are you, nuts?" They would think, probably not owing you the courtesy of responding out loud. They would walk off and mutter under their breath, "Some people just don't get it."

People do not enjoy the Grand Canyon because it makes us feel big. It doesn't do anything to enhance our self-esteem. It doesn't help us feel big. If anything, it makes us feel small. We are happy then. We are happiest when we feel small standing before something great.

Ever look at the stars? I do. I sometimes lay outside in the back yard on my trampoline and bask in the wonder of the bigness of space above a New Mexico desert. Scientists tell me that the light I see left those stars millions of years ago. The star itself could have gone out by now and we would still be seeing what looks like a star for millions of years. I feel small–and I love it.

> **People do not enjoy the Grand Canyon because it makes us feel big.**

You may say, "I can't do much." Neither can I. Each of us makes a small splash, but the rippling effect is huge. Because I have been working on this magnificent obsession for some time, I am profoundly aware of this. I have often said that I feel like one who is attempting to empty the Pacific Ocean with tea cups. Everyone I teach to double is one who did not know before. But there is so much to do.

Nobody knows for sure how many lost people inhabit planet earth, but to be sure, it is in the billions. There are likely more than a billion people who have never even heard of Jesus. A few billion more don't know any more about Jesus than you or I know about Confucius or Mohammed. They haven't really been given a fighting chance to believe. "How, then, can they call on the one they have not believed in? And how can they believe in the one of whom they have not heard? And how can they hear without someone preaching to them?" (Romans 10:14).

Billions.

The task is daunting. Tea cups trying to empty the Pacific. After we have doubled the number of God-worshiping people in the next 20 years, there will still be billions more to reach.

I feel small. But it feels good to feel small. It feels good to feel small, lost in a big, big cause. Lost in the big, big, cause of a big, big God.

What do you want to give your one and only life to? Do you want to give your life to collecting sea shells, playing softball, and trawling in your boat? Do you want to bury your talents and maintain the status quo? Or do you want to lose yourself in a big, big cause?

Join me. Give your life to the magnificent obsession of doubling. Lose yourself in the cause. It will make you happy.

But it is not just about making us happy. There is a much more serious, somber reason to double.

Reason #2: The Lostness of the Lost

The Bible teaches that those without Christ are headed to an eternally painful state of separation from God. Revelation 20 says, "And the devil, who deceived them, was thrown into the lake of burning sulfur, where the beast and the false prophet had been thrown. They will be tormented day and night forever and ever" (Rev. 20:10).

Tormented.

Tormented. Close the book and think about that word for sixty seconds.

Tormented. As I understand the broader context of scripture, the devil, the beast, and all those who do not call upon the name of the Lord will be tormented–day and night forever and ever.

> **They will be tormented day and night forever and ever. Rev. 20:10**

Tormented. The people on my cul-de-sac tormented day and night forever and ever. It is almost too much for me to bear.

I think we who are preachers shrink at times from speaking too loudly about this simply because it hurts too much. It is too horrible to repeat. Tormented day and night forever and ever.

We have the key to their escape. It is simple enough for a child to understand, yet profound enough to keep us pondering throughout eternity. We simply ask people to accept the fact that God accepts

13

them. We ask them to believe. We ask them to cooperate with what He is trying to do in their lives. It is as simple as A.B.C.

Accept the fact that God has accepted you.

Believe.

Cooperate with what God is trying to do in your life.

There are many who go to church their whole lives and don't grasp this simple reality. Becoming a Christian is not, at its core, about attending church, living by certain do's and don'ts, or performing certain rituals. It is about accepting the fact that God accepts me.

I have worked with some groups who do not believe in a literal hell. They believe that once you die, you die, and that is it. That is hard for me to believe in light of verses like this:

> **Becoming a Christian is not, at its core, about attending church, living by certain do's and don'ts or performing certain rituals.**

"There was a rich man who was dressed in purple and fine linen and lived in luxury every day. At his gate was laid a beggar named Lazarus, covered with sores and longing to eat what fell from the rich man's table. Even the dogs came and licked his sores.

"The time came when the beggar died and the angels carried him to Abraham's side. The rich man also died and was buried. In hell, where he was in torment, he looked up and saw Abraham far away, with Lazarus by his side. So he called to him, 'Father Abraham, have pity on me and send Lazarus to dip the tip of his finger in water and cool my tongue, because I am in agony in this fire.'

"But Abraham replied, 'Son, remember that in your lifetime you received your good things, while Lazarus received bad things, but now he is comforted here and you are in agony. And besides all this, between us and you a great chasm has been fixed, so that those who want to go from here to you cannot, nor can anyone cross over from there to us.'

Doubling is more fun than Six Flags, but this is not just fun and games.

"He answered, 'Then I beg you, father, send Lazarus to my father's house, for I have five brothers. Let him warn them, so that they will not also come to this place of torment.'

"Abraham replied, 'They have Moses and the Prophets; let them listen to them.'

" 'No, father Abraham,' he said, 'but if someone from the dead goes to them, they will repent.'

"He said to him, 'If they do not listen to Moses and the Prophets, they will not be convinced even if someone rises from the dead'" (Luke 16:19-31).

"I am in agony in this fire." Chilling.

People on your cul-de-sac and mine will soon be in agony in this fire. Doubling is more fun than Six Flags, but this is not just fun and games. Eternity is on the line. This is not a dress rehearsal. The enemy is shooting with real bullets.

To those who do not believe in a real, literal hell, I want to appeal to you. I disagree with you, but I still want to reach out to you. Would you agree with me that all eternity will be better for those who place their faith in Christ? Would you agree with me that all eternity will be unspeakably worse for those who don't place their faith in Christ? I know you would.

In contrast to hell, we read of heaven. Heaven: no more tears. No more crying. No more loneliness. No more fights. No more bills. No more bad weather. No more waiting. No more problems. No more children who break our hearts. Nothing but the pure, unmixed pleasure of joy in God. The Bible speaks of those who "long for his appearing" (2 Timothy 4:8). The longer I live, the more deeply I long for that day. As the old song says, "I am not at home in this world anymore." Heaven. What a contrast.

> **Eternity is on the line. This is not a dress rehearsal. The enemy is shooting with real bullets.**

Because it will make a difference for all eternity, I invite you to give your one and only life to the magnificent obsession of doubling your group every two years or less.

Reason #3: The Sickness in Our World

Where were you on September 11th, 2001? I was sitting in an airport. I will always remember. I am sure that you will never forget.

I will always remember and never forget sitting in the airport in Jacksonville, Florida and watching the second of the World Trade Center Towers collapse on live television. I will never forget. I wasn't aware at the time that the first tower had already fallen.

My first reaction was denial. "This can't happen," I protested in my mind. These are the World Trade Centers. I have been to New York City and seen these magnificent buildings. I thought they would be there on the New York skyline for the rest of my life.

I stayed in Jacksonville the rest of that week. I had a lot of time to sit in a hotel room and watch the news. I kept thinking, "What a sick world we live in."

Every time I see a schoolyard shooting I think to myself, "What a sick world we live in."

I have spoken at Wedgewood Baptist Church in Fort Worth, Texas where a few years ago a killer entered the building on a Wednesday night. The church was hosting a city-wide youth rally that night and the auditorium was packed with wild, adrenaline-charged teenagers. When the killer came in, everyone thought it was part of a skit for the night. They thought the bullets were loud, but surely loud blanks. They thought it was all a big drama until kids started falling to the ground in piles of blood. What a sick world we live in.

I was driving home from El Paso one night trying to keep myself awake by finding something on the radio that would keep my attention. I stopped on one station because I

> **I think the world is getting sicker, and I think we have the one and only cure.**

heard the city, "Jonesboro, Arkansas" mentioned. I have a brother who lives in this sleepy Arkansas town and was surprised to hear of Jonesboro on the news. You remember the story. You remember the schoolyard shooting. You remember the bloodshed. What a sick world we live in.

Our world can be changed. Jesus can change the hearts and minds of sick people. I invite you to join the magnificent obsession of doubling your group every two years or less because of the sickness in our world.

I think the world is getting sicker, don't you? I think the world is getting sicker, and I think we have the one and only cure. Politicians don't have the cure. Psychologists don't have the cure. Sociologists don't have the cure. The cure does not reside in better educational systems, better security systems, or better financial systems. There is no other cure.

What the world needs now is love, sweet love. The world even knows what the problem is. They know what the cure is. The cure is love.

> **What the world needs now is love, sweet love.**

They just don't know where to get it.

Here is how God's cure works. God pours his love into my broken heart. As my heart fills with His love, my heart begins to heal. Because God has cured my broken heart, I have the grace to put up with you! (Just kidding.) What I mean is, I have the grace to do what the Bible says when it commands us to "Bear with one another in love" (Colossians 3:13). And you have the grace to put up with me (no kidding) because God has filled your broken heart as well.

As I come to church with a full heart, full of God's love, I can come as Jesus came: not to be served, but to serve (Matthew 20:28). You too can come to serve, to give, to fill others' hearts. As many of us come to church with this perspective, the church becomes a hothouse of love, grace, and acceptance. We see the magic of the Christian life lived out before our eyes where people find their own cups being filled while filling the cups of others.

Out of this overflow of love, acceptance, and grace in the church, God's design is that we take that love to a world that so

Usually, love is sort of boring.

desperately needs it. With full hearts, we take love to a world that needs love poured into its broken hearts.

What is love, anyway? In church we often tell glorious and grandiose stories of the dramatic and sacrificial nature of love. Sometimes love is grandiose, dramatic, and sacrificial. Usually, however, it is not.

Usually, love is sort of boring. Love is sort of boring because life is sort of boring. Life–all of our lives–have a certain monotony to them that is, in a way, boring.

If I have lunch with someone I don't know very well, I might try to impress him with some exciting aspects of my life. But if we get to be friends, really good friends, he will discover that my life has a certain routine boringness to it. A lot of people think my life is exciting because I fly about 100,000 miles per year.

If you want to cure the disease that is in the world, you will be called upon to listen to the boring details of someone's boring, mundane life.

Sometimes, I do get to do and see some fun stuff. I got to see the Men's finals of the U.S. Open Tennis Tournament. I saw a sea turtle in the wild off the Great Barrier Reef, toured the Kennedy Space Center, went up into the St. Louis Arch, spent a day in the quaint little town of Avalon on Catalina Island, and visited the haunting grounds of the World Trade Center–and all that in the last 12 months.

Usually, however, it is another airport, another hotel room, another church. Just now I have a 3-hour lay over in Chicago O'Hare Airport. Big whup! The glories of air travel. Another airport.

But the people I love will ask me what I did and saw in the airport. They will ask me about the book I bought at the newsstand and the meal I ate at Chili's. People we love ask about the boring details of our lives.

If you want to cure the disease that is in the world, you will be called upon to listen to the boring details of someone's boring, mundane life. That is what

> **You don't have to pay off someone's mortgage to make them feel loved.**

love is and that is what life is like. It is a little bit boring. You love people by treating the details of their lives as really interesting.

When you love people in simple ways, like listening to them and inviting them to your home for Diet Coke, coffee cake, and cards, they feel thoroughly loved. When your group invites people to every fellowship every month, even if the fellowship is not that exciting, they will feel thoroughly loved. You don't have to pay off someone's mortgage to make her feel loved. Just treat her like a friend, like someone you care about, like a human being. Love people in ordinary, pedestrian ways and watch them come to love our Lord and receive His love into their lives.

Do you want to keep the Columbine tragedy from coming to your high school? Here is my advice. Don't concentrate so much on installing metal detectors at the entrances. Instead, concentrate on sending your students to the school on a mission. It is a mission of love. The mission is to love the outcast.

Every time you hear of a Columbine-type shooting, I invite you to listen for one word: outcast. "He was a good kid from a decent home, a good athlete, intelligent, but somewhat quiet and introverted, a bit of an outcast." Outcast. Challenge your kids to pour God's love into every outcast in their school. It is the greatest protection we have against the crazies. Love the crazies.

> "Hurt people hurt people," Rick Warren rightly reminds us.

"Hurt people hurt people," Rick Warren rightly reminds us. If there is anything in you that wants the hurting to stop, that wants the sickness in our world to be cured, that wants to give a better world to our children, I want to invite you to give your whole life to the magnificent obsession of doubling the church by doubling your class every two years or less.

Reason #4: Because of the Loneliness

Sociologists, looking at the culture in this generation, have said that "There is an epidemic of loneliness in our culture."[3] Perhaps loneliness occurs because we grew up in broken homes and didn't get the love, support, and nurturing we require. Perhaps because we move every four or five years and we never have the time to develop roots. Perhaps because we are just too darn busy.

Perhaps because we're letting Jerry Springer teach us how to get along with one another, and he is teaching us something that is contrary to scripture. While Jerry Springer incites his guests to anger and fights break out on stage, the Bible teaches that "A soft answer turns away wrath" (Proverbs 15:1). Proverbs teaches something very different from what Jerry Springer is teaching. Many in America have bought Jerry Springer's approach and others like it. The result is a profound loneliness.

> **The great need of the hour is not so much to tell the words about grace, but to be gracious to people.**

---

[3] Janet McCalman, "Welcome to the Age of Loneliness," *The Age* 9 Feb. 2002, 7 May 2003 http://www.theage.com.au/articles/2002/02/09/1013132463038.html

A basic missionary principle is to use the felt needs of a culture to reach that culture. If we find a culture that is hungry for physical bread, we find its people are far more likely to hear about the bread of life when we address their need for physical bread. In the same way, if we will love people in common, ordinary ways, they will be more likely to hear about Jesus, the lover of their souls. The great need of the hour is not so much to tell the words about grace, but to be gracious to people. People do need to hear the words about grace. "How can they believe unless they hear?" (Romans 10:14). But they will hear the words about grace as we are gracious to them.

> **Many who believe theologically in the tenant of grace are not very gracious.**

Many who believe theologically in the tenant of grace are not very gracious. They are just not very nice people. We need to be gracious, to live grace, to let grace flow through us, as well as talk about grace. Augustine said, "Share the gospel, and if you have to, use words."

One time I talked to a guy about doing a conference. We had all the details set up, and were about to hang up the phone, or so I thought. Then he asked, "Can I ask you a few questions?"

"Sure."

"Tell me about your theology. What do you believe?"

"Well, I grew up in a Baptist missionary and pastor's home. I was trained in two Baptist schools. I would describe my theology as in the mainstream of Baptist thought. If you want to go point by point, we can, but I am in the mainstream."

"What do you believe about _____? And what do you believe about_____?" (He mentioned a couple of hot potatoes in our denomination these days.)

"Well, I believe all the straight and narrow stuff about all that," I replied. But I wanted to ask, "What do you believe about the verse that says, 'Be ye kind one to another.'? Do you believe that

> **Augustine said, "Share the gospel, and if you have to, use words."**

is the holy, authoritative, inerrant word of almighty God? Because this doesn't feel like a lot of grace and kindness to me." There are too many angry, caustic, ungracious Christians. Those kind of Christians don't do a lot to cure the epidemic of loneliness that is in our culture.

Have you ever been lonely? Do you know what it feels like to be lonely? I never did–not until recently.

I grew up in a strong, nurturing, Christian home. I grew up as part of loving, Christian churches. I went to college and fell in with a group of guys who soon became the best of friends. We stood beside each other in our weddings and are still good friends to this day. I joined the staff at a church, and a staff member is the center of the social network. Because of this background, I had never been lonely.

I had never been lonely until I went through an unwanted, unwelcome, unexpected divorce. I got up one morning and Sharon handed me a note: "Read this, and I want us to talk about it." I read, "I am preparing to leave."

At the church where I was on staff, having this kind of marital problem was not allowed. It was a fire-able offense. And for good reason. The Bible says, "If anyone

> **Have you ever been lonely?**

does not know how to manage his own family, how can he take care of God's church?" (1 Tim. 3:5). They let me go. I am not debating whether it was a good idea to let me go. I am simply describing how I came to understand loneliness.

By the way, I ask you to refrain from thinking self-righteous and condemning thoughts about my Sharon or about me. Truth is, she has dealt with quite a bit of pain. I was not the ideal husband. I learned a lot, and she paid a dear price for some of my lessons. This is not about her. It's not even about all the mistakes I made. This is about me learning to understand loneliness.

There was actually a period of quite some time between my being let go by the church and Sharon leaving. During this period of time, my father-in-law passed away. I will never forget the night Sharon shook my feet to wake me and said two words, "Daddy died." I hugged her. We talked briefly. I started thinking through the logistics of making that four-hour drive to Roswell, New Mexico.

Then I remembered. Sharon's car was in the shop. My car had just gotten out of the shop. When I pulled it in the driveway, water was spewing everywhere. At the time, I thought, "Not to worry, I will let it cool off, fill it up with water, drive it back down to the shop, and let them fix it." I knew it would make it to the shop. But there was no way I could drive it four hours to Roswell to be with my mother-in-law who had just lost her husband.

When I left Calvary, I was disconnected from my supportive community. I remember sitting on my bed and crying, thinking, "I can't think of anyone who I feel comfortable calling at 3 a.m. and asking if I can borrow a car." Ever felt like that?

I went to Wal-mart in the middle of the night. Somewhat dazed, I told the salesman that my father-in-law just died and about my car problems. I asked if he possibly had anything I could use to fix it. We found a thing normally used to flush the radiator, but I was able to jerry-rig it to fix the problem. I will never forget the painful loneliness of that night.

Do you have any idea what deep loneliness feels like? Perhaps not. My guess is that many of you grew up in a strong, nurturing family and church, and you have never really been lonely. Can I tell you how it feels? It feels awful. We ought to be about the business of doubling our classes because of the epidemic of loneliness.

I remember my last day at work at Calvary. I had gone to work about 9 a.m., just as I had done most every day for the previous 11 years. I came home from work around 10:30 unemployed. At first I remember asking, "Well, when will this happen? It will take me a little while to hand off my responsibilities to others." The reply came, "You can leave right now."

I knew it would forever change my relationship with most of my friends at church. (You could argue that I didn't have the greatest attitude in the world, but I never felt that great about attending church there after they let me go.) That drive home was one of the darkest, loneliest moments of my life. I was losing my job, my ministry, my friends, my family, all in one fell swoop. As it turns out, Sharon decided to stay together for several more years, but I didn't know that at the time. It was a dark, gut-wrenching moment. Loneliness really hurts.

I remember after Sharon left I was driving one day with Destiny, my daughter, in the back seat of the car. Sharon was out of

> **Another thing I learned was that we serve a divorced God.**

town and she was crying for Momma. Destiny has always been a bit of a Momma's girl. "I want Momma. I want Momma. I want Momma." She cried and cried and cried. There was something about those words that resonated in my soul. "I want her too," I thought, "I want her so bad I could scream." I began to pound the steering wheel and flail and cry almost uncontrollably. I smashed the windshield with my fist. Thus is the pain of loneliness. It has driven me, at times, from being a basically happy, optimistic person to being almost suicidal.

Being single has not been all bad, by the way. It has made life much simpler. Sharon used to insist that I keep up with those little slips of paper and she would use them to balance the checkbook to the penny. I have never balanced the check book. I have never reconciled the checkbook. I just look on-line and see if I still have money.

I have only cooked one honest to goodness meal. When you don't cook, you don't have to buy groceries. You don't have to do dishes. I have only vacuumed the floor once in two years. (I do have a house cleaner come every two weeks.) I don't like it as well, but life is a lot simpler.

And I have learned a few lessons along the way. I have tasted the way much of the world lives and how painful loneliness can be. I have learned why God hates divorce (Malachi 2:16). I hate it too. I think everyone, especially those who have been through divorce, hates it. I would hate anything that would cause that kind of pain on one of my kids. I have told my kids over and over, "Whatever else you do in life, learn from my example. Keep your marriage together. Don't get divorced. It is awful."

> **God is pictured in the Bible as a jilted lover longing to reconcile with his bride.**

Another thing I learned is that we serve a divorced God. Jeremiah records, "I gave faithless Israel her certificate of divorce and sent her away because of all her adulteries" (Jeremiah 3:8). We served a divorced God. That is why God hates divorce. He has been there. He knows the pain.

God is pictured in the Bible as a jilted lover longing to reconcile with his bride. He asks us to join him in that process of reconciliation. That is why I want to double my class every two years or less.

I remember how happy I was when I finally got in a singles group and started to develop a group life again. What a wonderful way to live–in community. God has called us to not only have a relationship with Him. He has also called us to a relationship with one another. He has called us into community. What a wonderful way to live.

I have tasted loneliness like I never knew existed. I have tasted pain I didn't think was possible. Happily, some of you have likely never felt that pain, that loneliness. I want to bleed with you and tell you it is awful. Give yourself to the magnificent obsession of doubling your group every two years or less to do what you can to alleviate the loneliness that is in this world.

Reason #5: We Can Do It!

"I can do everything through Christ who strengthens me" (Philippians 4:13).

Can you double a class every two years or less through Christ who strengthens you? Can you? You can! And because we can, we should.

Someone asked George Leigh Mallory why he climbs mountains. "Because they are there." An equally good answer is, "Because we can."

Men are constantly challenged to live the adventure of trying new things, breaking new records, and boldly going where no one has gone before. Because we can, we should.

> **Whether we think we can or whether we think we cannot, either way we are right.**

Jesus said, "According to your faith it will be done for you" (Matthew 9:29). As Henry Ford said it, "Whether we think we can or whether we think we cannot, either way we are right."

It has only happened to me once, but one time someone came to me after a conference and said, "I just want you to know that what you talked about will not work in my setting." And do you know what? She is right. It won't work in her setting because she believes it won't work.

Henry Ford's words are true: whether you think you can or whether you think you cannot, either way you are right.

If you think it will be "us four, no more, same as before," guess what? It will be us four, no more, same as before. Jesus said it will be so. It will be done for you according to your faith. Whether you think you can or think you cannot, either way you are right.

> **Doubling every two years or less translates into going from 10 to 14 in a year.**

Because faith is so important, I would like to try to strengthen your faith and confidence that you can double your class in two years or less.

The average size group in the average church is 10. Some are larger, some are smaller, but the average is 10. Doubling every two years or less translates into 40% annual growth. It means going from 10 to 14 in a year. Ten to 14 in a year. If we can do that and do it on a consistent basis, we can turn our world upside down. It has become for me a magnificent obsession.

Imagine yourself in a typical Bible Study class or small group. Ten people are sitting around the living room or classroom at church. Imagine four empty chairs. If we can fill those four empty chairs in a year, we can turn our world upside down, double our class, double our church, and double the worldwide Church in the next twenty years.

We often get enamored by big things. We get enamored by watching big men break big piles of bricks. We get enamored by big campaigns and big buildings and big programs. I am not opposed to these things; they certainly can prove useful in advancing the kingdom of God.

I was in Australia recently and my host told me about his denomination renting the Sydney Opera Hall for 3 weeks for a series of evangelistic meetings at a price tag of three quarters of a million dollars. Big programs.

In this case, the big program resulted in very small results. My host went on to explain that if you were to look at a graph of the baptisms in the Sydney area, you would not be able to guess what year they rented the Opera Hall. Sometimes, when we do these big things there is more sizzle than steak.

Guess what I am enamored with. I am enamored with a Sunday School class that can go from 10 to 14 in a year. If we can do that and do it consistently, we can turn the world upside down.

I would actually like to challenge you to a slightly higher goal: to thoroughly assimilate two people per class per quarter.

The McDonald's Corporation has always fascinated me. My first real job was at McDonald's, and I was introduced early to some of the amazing feats of this mammoth company. According to Michael Gerber's research, one out of every sixteen dollars that we spend in America at restaurants we spend at McDonald's.[4]

How are McDonald's corporate staff able to do it? Pretty simple. They have figured out a way to take a 16-year old kid, whose parents cannot get him to clean up his room, and teach him to deliver hot, fresh, lightly salted french fries in less than two minutes at a reasonable price in a clean store. And because they are able to do that every single time, they can rule the hamburger world.

All of the energy of the McDonald's Corporation is focused down to this one simple task: to take a 16 year old kid, whose parents cannot get him to clean up his room, and teach him to deliver hot, fresh, lightly salted french fries in less than two minutes at a reasonable price in a clean store.

Now, let me define my terms: a thoroughly assimilated person is a person whose name is scribbled on the back of half a dozen member's phone books.

In a similar way, if we can focus all our energy to this simple task, teaching a Bible Study teacher to double every two years or less, we can win our world for Christ. All we have to do to double is go from 10 to 14 in a year.

---

[4]Michael Gerber, *The E-Myth Revisited* (New York: HarperBusines, 1995) 81.

But I challenge you to a slightly higher goal. Here it is: thoroughly assimilate two people per class per quarter. There you have it, the secret to world evangelization: to thoroughly assimilate two people per class per quarter.

This breaks down the cause of world evangelization into a bite-sized plan that we can sink our teeth into. All we have to do is to thoroughly assimilate two people per class per quarter.

Now, let me define my terms: a thoroughly assimilated person is a person whose name is scribbled on the backs of half a dozen members' phone books. This is not just a name on a class role. This is not just someone who I am vaguely aware of. This is someone who has been in my home, who knows my dog, with whom I have gone to the beach. (Out in New Mexico, where I live, we have a beach, but no ocean. It is called White Sands.) This is someone with whom I have laughed and cried.

If we can thoroughly assimilate two new people per class per quarter, we can turn the world upside down. We can. And because we can, we should. We can, through Christ who strengthens us.

Without Christ, we can do nothing. John 15 teaches us that except we abide in the vine, we can bear no fruit. Not just a little fruit. No fruit. Without Christ, we can do nothing. But with Christ, we can do all things. We can double our classes, double our churches, and see the worldwide Church double in the next 20 years through Christ who strengthens us.

We can, but we must want it. It will not come to us easily. It will be hard work. It will come to us when it becomes a magnificent obsession.

Through Christ, We Really *Can* Do It

In my book, *You Can Double Your Class in Two Years or Less*[5], I detail a plan for doubling a group. Let me overview that content. Here are the five steps to double a class every two years or less:

T -   **Teach a half-way decent lesson each and every week; nothing less will do.** You do not have to be Chuck Swindoll to grow a class. However, you must produce reasonably good lessons every single week in order to grow a class. The better the teaching, the easier it is to grow a class. Some teachers are so good at teaching they can grow a class on the sheer magnetism of their presentation. You are probably not that good. Not many are. But you are probably good enough, or you can be. Strive to teach as well as you can. The number one predictor of the growth of a class is the teaching ability of the teacher.

---

[5]Josh Hunt, *You Can Double Your Class in Two Years or Less* (Loveland, CO: Group, 1997).

I have been asking groups recently, "Think back over a life of attending Sunday School. What percentage of the teachers you have listened to would you say drop below the bar of half-way decent? In other words, in what percentage of the groups you have attended is the teaching so bad that it will greatly hinder the ability of that group to double?" The answer that comes back varies widely according to personal experience, but the average is about a third. One-third of the teachers who we have heard over the years drop below the bar of half-way decent teaching.

> **One third of the teachers whom we have heard over the years drop below the bar of half-way decent teaching.**

A friend told me about one such group. The teacher walked in and announced, "I didn't get a chance to get to my lesson this week." He turned to the person on his left, "Would you read page one out of our quarterly?" He looked at the person sitting next to him, "Would you read the next page?" and so forth around the room. "When we get to page seven, we will have prayer requests, close in prayer, and we will be done." Let me make a couple of comments about this.

First, if you can't teach any better than that, please quit. There are many wonderful ways to serve God. Teaching is only one. We will look at several others shortly. God has gifted you; there are things you can do. Teaching may not be one of them. For the sake of your class, please quit. For the sake of the kingdom, please quit.

Second, you could spend a million dollars advertising that class, and you wouldn't get it to grow. You could have a hundred trained, gifted evangelists attached to that group, and it wouldn't grow. As someone in Oklahoma told me, "Good visitation will not overcome bad teaching."

> **Good visitation will not overcome bad teaching.**

It is a sin against God to bore people with the gospel. It is a sin against God and man to take the greatest news ever to hit planet Earth and present it in such a way that people get the idea that it is boring. As Howard Hendricks is fond of saying, "If you want to bore them, bore them with earth science, bore them with math. But don't take the greatest news ever to hit planet Earth and bore people with it."

We have to have half-way decent teaching each and every week; nothing less will do.

If you choose to teach, I invite you to join me in making a promise. Promise me you will get better. I love teaching, and for that reason I have made a promise to God. For the rest of my life, as long as I get to teach, I am going to try to get better and better at it. I invite you to make a similar promise. For as long as you get to teach, resolve to get better and better and better at teaching.

Every teacher could benefit from going through some of the following courses:

- Howard Hendricks' video series, *The Seven Laws of the Teacher.*

- Bruce Wilkinson's *The Seven Laws of the Teacher* and *Teaching with Style.*

- Bert Decker's *Communicating with Bold Assurance.*

- My own series, *Disciplemaking Teachers.*

- Rick Warren's *Purpose Driven Preaching and Teaching.*

The Scripture says, "Of making many books there is no end" (Eccles. 12:12b). When you finish these courses, there will be a slew of other courses that can help you be a better teacher. Take those courses. Teach those courses. If you really want to be better, teach a course on teaching.

The #1 predictor of the growth of any group is the quality of the teaching. If you are the teacher, promise me you will get better.

I - **Invite every member and every visitor to every fellowship every month.** If we love them, they will come. We invite every member because it is good inreach. We invite every visitor, because it is good outreach. We do it every month because it is effective ministry.

Don't invite people to class. Instead, invite them to the party.

If you want to double your group, my invitation to you is, "Don't invite people to class. Instead, invite them to the party." I have seen it happen more times than I can count: if I can get them to the party, I cannot keep them from the class.

Why? There is an epidemic of loneliness out there. People don't have a dozen names scribbled on the outside of their phone books. They don't have people to call in times of stress or grief, or if they just feel like seeing someone. They are lonely. And when we love people in common, ordinary, pedestrian ways, like inviting them to the party, they respond. Love is an irresistible offer.

As I said earlier, love can be a little bit boring. What I mean is this: we talk about the routine, boring details of our lives with the people we love. If you want to communicate to someone that you care about him, you don't have to pay off his mortgage. You can do it by inviting every member and every prospect to every fellowship every month.

> **People who are opposed to the gospel are not opposed to ice cream.**

Ultimately, the fellowship is not about the fellowship, but about the fellowship. If you have a bowling fellowship, it is not about bowling. It is about the fellowship that happens while someone else is bowling. Fellowship is about talking and listening to the routine details of one another's lives.

G - **Give Friday nights to Jesus for an informal time of fellowship, cards, and Diet Coke.** People who are opposed to the gospel are not opposed to ice cream. The Bible says, "Offer hospitality to one another without grumbling" (I Peter 4:9). If we will simply be obedient to this one command, we can double our classes every two years or less and our churches every five years or less.

"Friday nights" is a metaphor. It is a metaphor for an informal time of Diet Coke, coffee cake, and card playing. It is a metaphor for whatever you like to do. My invitation to you is to get systematic and consistent about inviting people to join you in doing whatever you enjoy doing.

I have taught this "Friday Nights" plan all across America and Australia with very positive feedback. One man in Florida told me he is hitting 100%. Every single person he has had in his home and fed his coffee cake to has joined his church. Another man in Ohio told he was hitting 97%. Ninety-seven percent of the people he had in his home have joined his church. (I think this guy likes to play on spreadsheets.) It works in California. Someone there told me 9 out of 10 people he had in his home joined his church. Oklahoma: same thing–9 out of 10.

There has only been one time when the giving Friday nights to Jesus plan did not work. I talked to one guy who said, "I read your book; love your book; love the 'giving Friday nights to Jesus plan.'"

"Great!" I asked, "How is it going?"

"Oh, I don't do it. I just think it is a great idea."

In this case, for some reason, it didn't work.

I sat next to a guy once who described his job as training the top real estate agents in the top agencies in the top markets all across the country. I asked what separated the race horses from the rest of the pack at that level? Are they smarter? Better looking? Do they do different things than the rest of the pack?

"Not really," he replied. Everyone knows how to be successful. Success leaves clues. It is common knowledge what you have to do to be successful in nearly any field. These race horses do the same things that others do, they just do them every single time. They have reduced these success steps to systems and checklists, and they do the same things that everyone else does–but consistently.

Giving Friday nights to Jesus will have unexpected benefits. You'll get to know people you otherwise wouldn't. Once we had a friend who reciprocated and invited us into his home. I will never forget the night John welcomed me into his home. He asked, "Can I get you something to drink? We have Diet Coke, Dr. Pepper, and cold beer." Calmly, I asked for a Diet Coke. But inside, I was exuberant. "A real, live, pagan!" I thought. No Baptist I know would expect a Baptist minister to drink cold beer in public!

I want to invite you to systematically and consistently invite every member and every prospect to every fellowship every month.

E -   **Encourage the group toward ministry.** We do this by providing specific examples of ministry and personally enlisting people to join the team. I encourage people to pick from the following seven examples of ministry opportunities:

- **Teacher.** Bookish students, these individuals love to study and present truth. Most churches need more teachers. All churches need more teachers of kids. In a way, it is an unfortunate title, teacher. It implies that all this person does is teach. He or she is like the pastor of the class. The pastor teaches, but he does more than teach. He also oversees the overall affairs of the church. Similarly, the teacher serves as a leader in the church and sees that the group functions in a healthy way.

- **Outreach leader.** Extroverted and outwardly focused, these soldiers see that we invite every prospect to every fellowship every month.

- **Inreach leader.** Parent-like and caring, kind and compassionate, these people notice. They notice when people are not present. When people are not missed, they miss. Inreach leaders see that people are missed. They call. They write. They care. They invite every member to every fellowship every month.

- **Fellowship leader(s).** Normally, this is several people–several highly social people who love doing things together. If you ask any one person to plan a party, she will turn you down so fast it will make your head spin. But ask three people to help, and they will plan a party to plan the parties.

- **Hospitality leader** (gives Friday nights to Jesus).

- **Prayer leader.** The fastest church growth story I know is a church in Georgia that doubled in about 6 months, going from about 200 to about 400 in half a year. How did they do it? Prayer. (Has it come to that?) More specifically, they got organized around the idea that everyone was called every week to see if they had any prayer needs. People felt so cared for that the church grew, and grew rapidly.

- **Class leader.** If you have someone in your group who carries a Palm or similar hand- held Personal Digital Assistant, they make an excellent candidate for class leader. People who carry Palms don't do any actual work. They just delegate, supervise, oversee, and coordinate. Most of us need someone like that. We have good intentions, but we don't get around to it. Leaders see that everyone gets around to it. People without the gift for leadership feel guilty every time they ask someone to do something. They think, "I could just do it myself." Leaders don't suffer from this guilt. They realize that asking other people to work is work in itself.

Detailed job descriptions are provided in *You Can Double Your Class in Two Years or Less.*

You may be thinking that this is a book for Sunday School teachers. It is more. It is not a book just for Sunday School teachers because teachers normally are not equipped to do everything. That is why God created the body of Christ. That is why I am fond of saying,

"Each one use his gifts to grow your group to double your class every two years or less."

You can do things your teacher can't do. Your teacher needs you. Your group needs you. Maybe you can plan parties, or keep up with the people whose names appear on the class role. Perhaps you are an extroverted person who doesn't mind mixing with outsiders. We need you. Perhaps you have a heart for prayer. We need you to be involved with your group, using your gifts toward the goal of doubling every two years or less. It's about building a community, and everyone serves a vital role. It needs to become a magnificent obsession.

R -   **Reproduce.** Doubling a class every two years or less is not about going from ten to twenty. It is about going from one group to two. Reproduction is hard on any level. Still, the future of the church is the reproduction of groups. The key to creating a new group is leadership. The price of creating a new group is saying good-bye. We must be willing to say good-bye in order to be obedient to the Great Commission.

It is hard to say good-bye. It is hard for missionaries going oversees to say good-bye to family and friends left behind. I know. When my parents announced that they were taking the family half-way around the globe to serve as missionaries in the Philippines, my grandparents' response was curt and clear: "NO!" My parents' eyes widened. They heard, "No you are not! You are not taking my grandbabies 10,000 miles from home to be raised in the jungles of the Philippines.

We will not miss their next four birthdays." The price of saying good-bye is extremely high.

I am not necessarily asking you to fly across an ocean and raise your family in the tropics. I am asking you to leave some of your best friends for one hour a week to help start a new class. This will be a higher price than some are willing to pay for the advancement of the kingdom. This is why we must produce mature disciples with a kingdom mentality. Only the mature can reproduce. Only mature disciples are willing to say good-bye. We must reproduce in order to ensure the life of the next generation.

I had someone disagree with me at this point. A lady stood up in a seminar in Ohio and said, "I disagree, Josh; I like big groups."

Eventually, growth will kill a small group.

"How big?"

"Oh, big. . . maybe 40."

"O.K., a little big for my taste, but go with 40. Suppose God answers your prayers and you double every two years or less, where will you be in two years?"

"80."

"Suppose God answers your prayers again. Suppose you double again. Where will you be in two more years?"

"160."

That is not a small group anymore. It is a church. It is about twice the size of the average church.

Eventually, growth will kill a small group. What I mean is that if a small group grows, somewhere along the line it will not be small anymore.

I have another work called *T.I.G.E.R. Training: Eight Things Teachers Must Have from their Pastor and Staff to Double Every Two Years or Less*[6]. In this work, I detail 10 ways to start new groups. We don't have time to retrace that here. I simply want to invite you to give your life to doubling every two years or less.

We really can do it. And because we can, we should.

---

[6]Josh Hunt, *T.I.G.E.R. Training: Eight Things Teachers Must Have from their Pastor and Staff to Double Every Two Years or Less*, video, 2020 Vision.

Reason #6: The Power of Multiplication

Imagine you were to take an ordinary piece of paper and fold it once, twice, three times–fifty times. This is actually impossible because before long the paper will be so small you can't keep folding it. Still, imagine you could. How thick do you think the resulting piece of paper would be?

As thick as a big city phone book?

As tall as a refrigerator? That is what my son thought.

The correct answer is roughly the distance from the earth to the sun. This is the power of multiplication.

Can't believe it? Imagine this. Suppose I am right. How thick would the stack of paper be if we folded it fifty-one times? Roughly the distance from the earth to the sun and back, right? This is the power of multiplication. This is why I am enamored by small things. "Who has despised the day of small things?" (Zechariah 4:10). Not me, because I know that small things can lead to huge things.

This is the divinely ordained strategy modeled for us through the apostle Paul. Every teacher should aspire to say this to a member of his or her group:

> And the things you have heard me say in the presence of many witnesses entrust to reliable men who will also be qualified to teach others. (2 Tim. 2:2)

Note that the things that were imparted were not imparted one-on-one. This verse is often used to support a one-on-one discipleship ministry. I am not opposed to such a ministry. I just want to be quick to point out that this is not what this verse is talking about. This verse is not talking about one-on-one. This verse is talking about the church living out church life in the context of a group.

We don't know how big of a group it was. Perhaps it was 10. Perhaps it was 200. We don't know. The text doesn't say. I tend to eat, breathe, and sleep group life, so I think it in terms of a small group. I think of Paul speaking to Timothy and ten or so others in a small group. Then turning to Timothy saying, "The things we have been talking about–living the Christian life–I want you to impart to another group. In that group, find a leader that can start another group and find another leader, and so forth until the whole earth is full of His glory. It is my magnificent obsession."

Pictured graphically, it looks like this. Imagine Paul said this, not only to Timothy, but to at least three others who imparted these truths in the context of ten or more. How many are impacted in the first generation?

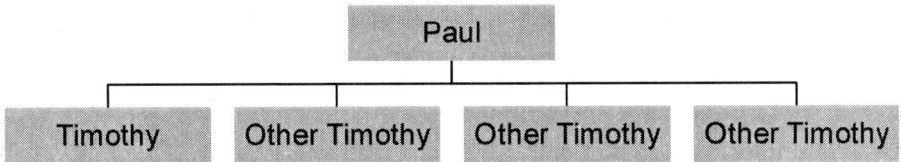

Suppose that Timothy and these 3 other Timothies multiplied. Suppose each one started 4 other groups of ten. How many are being impacted at this point?

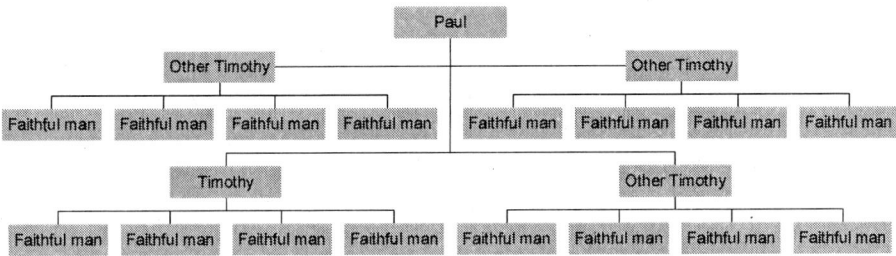

But Paul didn't stop there. He said, "The things you have heard me say. . . impart to faithful men who will also be qualified to teach others. Do the math here. How many little boxes do you see here? Suppose each one of these boxes represents a group of 10 people, how many people are being impacted?

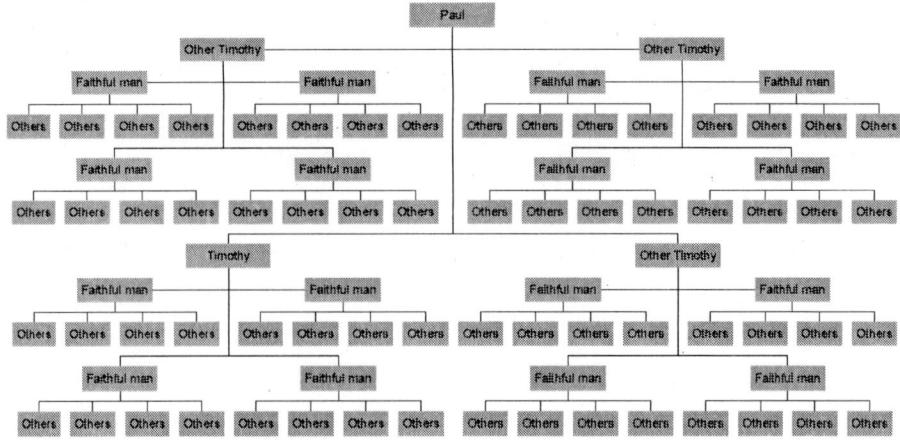

The correct answer is 850. That is the power of multiplication.

Perhaps you are thinking that you do not have these large, grandiose visions for your life. I invite you to accept such a vision! I invite you to give your life to the magnificent obsession of doubling every two years or less because through the power of multiplication, fantastic results can occur.

Jesus told us a parable about a seed that fell among four soils. He interpreted the parable as follows:

> When anyone hears the message about the kingdom and does not understand it, the evil one comes and snatches away what was sown in his heart. This is the seed sown along the path. The one who received the seed that fell on rocky places is the man who hears the word and at once receives it with joy. But since he has no root, he lasts only a short time. When trouble or persecution comes because of the word, he quickly falls away.

The one who received the seed that fell among the thorns is the man who hears the word, but the worries of this life and the deceitfulness of wealth choke it, making it unfruitful. But the one who received the seed that fell on good soil is the man who hears the word and understands it. He produces a crop, yielding a hundred, sixty or thirty times what was sown. (Matthew 13:19-23)

Question: what three qualities described the good soil? (I am a small group leader at heart; go ahead, indulge me–what three qualities describe the good soil?)

The good soil is the soil that hears the word of God. Truthfully all the soils hear the word of God. The second quality of the good soil is that it understood the word. There was at least one other soil that understood. But there was a third quality of the good soil, did you find it? The good soil produced a crop. Jesus said in another place. "I am the vine; you are the branches. If a man remains in me and I in him, he will bear much fruit; apart from me you can do nothing" (John 15:5). If we remain in Him and are good soil, we will bear fruit. We produce a crop. And what kind of crop? Did you pick up on that? A big crop or little crop? What kind of crop? "One hundred, sixty, or thirty times what was sown."

This is one of the most convicting verses in all the Bible to me. Jesus is saying we produce a crop, and a big crop, or else. . .

Or else we are bad soil. I told you it was one of the most convicting verses in all the Bible. We produce a big crop or we are bad soil. Ouch. Thank God for grace.

One of the best ways I know to produce good soil is through multiplying groups.

I think of my friend, Larry Mays. I think on a time 20 years ago. He is teaching and reproducing what he has been given. About 25 or 30 people sit before him. Ten years later, 25 or 30 people sit before him.

But about three years into this story, Larry reproduced himself in a man also named Larry. He says to Larry, "Larry, I believe in you. I think you could be a Sunday School teacher. I have heard the way you answer questions. I have seen the way you live. I have sensed your heart for God. I want to ask you to start substituting for me. Over time, I am going to gradually hand the reigns of this group to you, and I am going to go off and teach something else to somebody else." At the ten year point, Larry #2 was teaching to 25 or 30 and Larry #1 was still teaching to 25 or 30.

About the seven year point, Larry found another "Timothy." His name was Mike. He said to Mike, "Mike, I believe in you. I think you could be a Sunday School teacher. I have heard the way you answer questions. I have seen the way you live. I have sensed your heart for God. I want to ask you to start substituting for me. Over time, I am going to gradually hand the reigns of this group to you, and I am going to go off and teach something else to somebody else."

After 10 years, Larry was ministering to 80 people a week. Twenty five or so in his group, and about the same number in two other groups. Larry produced a crop. What kind of crop? A big crop. I want to invite you to create a big crop too! The best way I know to do that is through multiplying groups.

Through the power of multiplication we can turn the world upside down.

Through the power of multiplication we can reach our world for God and offer it to Him as a thank offering for all He has done for us.

Through the power of multiplication we can see our wildest dreams for the kingdom realized.

You will not be able to build buildings fast enough. You will not be able to start services fast enough. You will not be able to birth new churches fast enough. Nothing can stop a movement of God where groups are doubling every two years or less.

If we can focus all of our energy toward a group and teach that group to go from 10 to 14 in a year, the world is our oyster. We can fulfill our wildest ministry dreams through the power of multiplication and groups that are doubling every two years or less.

Reason #7: Because of the Joy

People with great joy in God have great energy for God. They accomplish great things for God.

The joy of the Lord is our strength (Nehemiah 8:10). It is our fuel. It is our energy. The church is languishing today, not because we cannot figure out how to double a class every two years or less. We are languishing because we do not have the energy to do so. The energy comes from joy.

The problem we face in the church is not a methodological problem. It is not that we do not know how to double a group every two years or less. It is a theological problem.

> **People with great joy in God have great energy for God. They accomplish great things for God.**

It is widely taught in the church today that feelings don't matter. What matters is behavior. You can feel up, down, glad, sad, or mad. We don't really care. We just want you to believe right and behave right.

It shows up in the titles of some of our best selling books. These books have some great content, but taken the wrong way, we can get the wrong idea from the titles. *Love is a Decision,* and *Love is Choice.* Implication: what matters is decisions and choices; feelings don't really matter. Feelings are optional.

There was a book that came out several years ago by one of my favorite writers, Dr. James Dobson. The book is titled *Feelings, Can You Trust Them?* Bottom line: you can't trust them. But, if you don't read carefully, you could get the idea that Dr. Dobson is saying that feelings don't matter, that you can feel up, down, glad, sad, or mad. It doesn't matter. What matters is what you *do.*

I heard a similar teaching four times last summer. One book on Christian marriage said, "God's purpose in Christian marriage is not to make you happy; it is to make you holy." Another well known writer spoke of Joseph, saying, "God's purpose in Joseph's life was to make him holy, not to make him happy." One teacher said it more strongly, "God doesn't care a flip about your happiness. What He cares about is your holiness." It is not true. God does care about our happiness just as surely as we as parents care about our kids' happiness. It makes dramatic preaching to proclaim, "God doesn't care about your happiness. He cares about your holiness." It makes good preaching, but bad theology. God does care; in fact, He commands our happiness.

> There is no holiness except that there is obedience to the command of a holy God to "Rejoice in the Lord."

The really disturbing thing about happiness versus holiness teaching is that it implies that we have to choose between the two. We either choose happiness, in which case we can't be holy. Or we choose holiness, in which case we cannot possibly be happy. Nothing could be further from the truth. We do not have to choose between happiness and holiness. In fact, they necessarily come together.

There is no holiness without obedience to the command of holy God to "Rejoice in the Lord." And there is no true, lasting, abiding happiness without holiness. There is merely passing pleasure.

Paul repeated it three times to the Philippian church for emphasis. Rejoice in the Lord. Rejoice in the Lord. Rejoice in the Lord.

In a day when they didn't have various size and style fonts, bold, italics, and underlining. In a day when they didn't use pull quotes for emphasis, they used repetition for emphasis. Paul wrote about a quarter of the New Testament. He wanted to make sure we didn't miss this important command in the mass of teaching. This is an important one.

Paul describes joy as a "safeguard." It is like those guardrails along mountainous roads that protect us from going to the ravine below. They protect us because we are hard-wired for joy. We can't avoid it. We can't deny it. We can't get away from it. We are hard-wired for joy. We either find joy in God, or we find joy in this world's meager offerings, but one way or another, we have to find joy.

The Psalmist attached the most outrageous promise to this command: "Delight yourself in the Lord and he will give you the desires of your heart" (Psalm 37:4). God tells us that He will give us whatever we want if we will just get happy in Him.

What was it that frustrated God about the people of Israel in the wilderness? They wouldn't get happy. They were constantly murmuring, complaining, and grumbling. Paul offers a severe warning based on their experience: "And do not grumble, as some of them did–and were killed by the destroying angel" (1 Cor. 10:10). Do you hear how serious God is about getting happy? He warns us, "Get happy, or I just might have to kill you."

I taught on this in a small group once and had one person respond in a somber, dead-faced tone: "I am happy. I am very, very happy." I wanted to say, "Well, tell your face!"

Do you remember how happy the early church was? They were so happy that when outsiders came in, the outsiders thought they were drunk! They had a visible happiness. Is it true of your church?

People who have great joy in God have great energy for God and accomplish great things for God.

I talked to a guy once on an airplane. He asked me what I do. I explained that I do seminars for churches. "What kind of churches?" "Oh, mostly Baptist churches, sometimes other groups have me in."

> "A happy Christian." He paused, seemingly a bit puzzled. "I have never met a happy Christian."

"Oh, so you are a Christian, then?" he queried. (I thought this was obvious by this point.) "Yes," I beamed, "and a happy Christian."

I will remember what he said next for the rest of my life. "A happy Christian." He paused, seemingly a bit puzzled. "I have never met a happy Christian."

"Well, you have now. I am just as happy as a little clam to be a Christian."

In reflecting on that conversation, I thought, "Where would we be as a Christian movement if the world looked at us and said, 'I am not sure about many of your teachings, but you people are so incredibly happy!'?" Where would we be toward the goal of doubling the Church if the world looked at us, unsure of the trustworthiness of our Bible, but convinced beyond the shadow of a doubt that we Christians are the happiest people they have ever met.

In my book, *Enjoying God*[7], we explore six steps to becoming obedient to the command of a holy God to rejoice in the Lord always. Allow me to overview those steps. They spell the word L.E.A.D.E.R.

Learn to live the well-lived life. The first lie of the church is that feelings don't matter. The second lie is that circumstances don't matter. We scold the man who says, "I am doing pretty well under the circumstances." We are admonished to live above the

> **The first lie of the church is that feelings don't matter. The second lie is that circumstances don't matter.**

circumstances. Like any good lie, there is a little truth in this. James 1:2 commands us to count it all joy when we face trials of various kinds. That is the pinnacle, the high water-mark of Christian maturity. When

---

[7]Josh Hunt, *Enjoying God*, (Las Cruces, NM: 2020 Vision, 2001).

we reach the ability to throw a party when all hell breaks loose, we know we have reached the mountain of spiritual maturity. We need to lean in that direction.

But on the way, we need to learn another skill: get our lives together. It is easier to enjoy God in the context of a well-lived life. In as much as it depends on you, live at peace with all men (Romans 12:18). It is easier to enjoy God when you have enough money rather than when you run out. That is why the writer of Proverbs said, "Give me neither poverty nor riches, but give me only my daily bread. Otherwise, I may have too much and disown you and say, 'Who is the Lord?' Or I may become poor and steal, and so dishonor the name of my God" (Proverbs 30:8-9).

> **It is easier to enjoy God in the context of a well-lived life.**

We need to do two things simultaneously. Number one, we need to get our lives together. Number two, we need to learn to rejoice in a life that is not all together.

Express your joy in God in worship. Some of the happiest times in my life have been times of worship. I have come to understand what the hymn writer had in mind when he wrote, "Sweet hour of prayer, sweet hour of prayer." People who enjoy God enjoy long, leisurely times of worship. They love to sing. They love to shout.

I recently saw a sign in the children's area of a church. It read, "I will be quiet in church." How different from what we read in scriptures: "Praise him with the trumpet and with lute and harp. Praise him with the drums and dancing. Praise him with stringed instruments and horns. Praise him with the cymbals, yes, loud clanging cymbals" (Psalm 150:3-5; LIVING)

People who enjoy God love music. They love to listen to loud, joyous music. They invest heavily in music that causes their heart to sing.

Attack the enemy. There is a war going on. Whether we like it or not, there is a war going on. We can wake up and smell the coffee and recognize we are in a war, or we can bury our head in the sand and get our backsides kicked. Either way, there is a war.

> **Some of the happiest times in my life have been times of worship.**

The Bible clearly teaches that ours in an offensive battle. The Bible says "The gates of hell will not prevail against us." Gates are defensive. They don't move. The implication is we are attacking the enemy.

Paul told us to put on the full armor of God. Interestingly, all of the armor is offensive armor. We are not told of any armor to protect the backside. We have a breastplate of righteousness, but we have no backplate.

The happiest people I know are group leaders who are attacking the enemy by doubling their group every two years or less.

Do the things God has called you to do. Joy is in the doing. It is not only in the relating. It is not only in the knowing. It is also in the doing. There is nothing like the thrill of discovering what God has called you to do and doing it with all your might. The happiest people on the planet are not the people surrounded by luxury and ease and every kind of creature comfort. The happiest people on the planet are people who are lost in a grand cause. They are doing the things God has called them to do. They are exhausted in the battle and loving every minute of it.

Express your joy in God to others. Expressing joy is not only a reaction to joy, it is a part of joy. What fun is it to win the game, sink the putt, or make the deal if you can't tell someone about it? Joy is in the telling.

> **The quality of life is largely dependant on the quality of relationships.**

Relate to others in healthy relationships. The quality of life is largely dependant on the quality of relationships. If you have good relationships, you have a good life. If you have poor relationships, life is pretty hard.

These six steps lead us to be people who have the energy of joy to pursue our magnificent obsession.

Reason #8: Because Jesus Told Us To

When I was growing up, I used to like to sleep in on Saturdays. My mom would often leave a list sitting on the breakfast bar. "Mow the lawn. Take out the trash. Do the dishes." You know the drill.

Imagine Mom came back after several hours. I meet her at the door, "Momma, Momma, I found your note sitting on the breakfast bar. I want you to know, Momma, how carefully I have been reading, meditating on, and memorizing the words you put here on this legal pad. I have been pondering your intent as you penned the words, 'Mow the lawn. Take out the trash. Do the dishes.' I have looked up quite a number of these words in their original etymology. Momma, you will be happy to know that I can tell you the whole history of the lawn mower.'"

How would your momma respond?

This ain't rocket science what God asked us to do. He asked us to go, make disciples of all nations (Matthew 28:19). Make disciples. Not hold meetings or do visitation or have classes. Not hold meetings except those meetings that help us to reach people for Christ and make disciples of them.

I have heard many say, "I believe in slow, steady growth. I believe in slow, steady growth because I believe slow, steady growth is healthy growth. Well, that sounds good to me. I like healthy growth too. The trouble is that that is not what the Bible says. What kind of growth did Paul want? What kind of growth did he pray for? You make the call:

> Finally, brothers, pray for us that the message of the Lord may spread rapidly and be honored, just as it was with you. (2 Thes. 3:1)

Paul prayed for rapid growth, and my heart's desire is that the church would grow rapidly.

Consider the following passage. Underline the word "double" each time you read it.

> "Again, the Kingdom of Heaven can be illustrated by the story of a man going on a trip. He called together his servants and gave them money to invest for him while he was gone. He gave five bags of gold to one, two bags of gold to another, and one bag of gold to the last—dividing it in proportion to their abilities—and then left on his trip. The servant who received the five bags of gold began immediately to invest the money and soon doubled it. The servant with two bags of gold also went right to work and doubled the money. But the servant who received the one bag of gold dug a hole in the ground and hid the master's money for safekeeping.

> Sir, you gave me five bags of gold to invest, and I have doubled the amount.

"After a long time their master returned from his trip and called them to give an account of how they had used his money. The servant to whom he had entrusted the five bags of gold said, 'Sir, you gave me five bags of gold to invest, and I have doubled the amount.' The master was full of praise. 'Well done, my good and faithful servant. You have been faithful in handling this small amount, so now I will give you many more responsibilities. Let's celebrate together!'

"Next came the servant who had received the two bags of gold, with the report, 'Sir, you gave me two bags of gold to invest, and I have doubled the amount.' The master said, 'Well done, my good and faithful servant. You have been faithful in handling this small amount, so now I will give you many more responsibilities. Let's celebrate together!'

"Then the servant with the one bag of gold came and said, 'Sir, I know you are a hard man, harvesting crops you didn't plant and gathering crops you didn't cultivate. I was afraid I would lose your money, so I hid it in the earth and here it is.'

"But the master replied, 'You wicked and lazy servant! You think I'm a hard man, do you, harvesting crops I didn't plant and gathering crops I didn't cultivate? Well, you should at least have put my money into the bank so I could have some interest. Take the money from this servant and give it to the one with the ten bags of gold. To those who use well what they are given, even more will be given, and they will have an abundance. But from those who are unfaithful, even what little they have will be taken away. Now throw this useless servant into outer darkness, where there will be weeping and gnashing of teeth.'" (Matthew 25:14-30; NLT)

Let's do a little Bible Study together. Answer these four questions, will you?

1.   What did the "good and faithful" servants do?

2.   What did the "wicked, lazy" servant do?

3.   What happened to the servant who doubled?

4.   What happened to the servant who did not double?

I don't know about you, but I want to be the good and faithful servant, the servant who doubles. I don't want to be the servant who takes what he has been given and does not double it. I want to do all I can to help my group double and I want to do all I can to help others double. It has become, for me, a magnificent obsession.

Reason #9: Because It Is a Reasonable Response to All God Has Done for Us

I was vacationing once on the east coast. It was a big family reunion, a potluck dinner. It was by a body of water, and there was a small pier that jetted out into the water. I was out there on the little pier, along with my two boys, Dawson and Dustin. Dustin was about a year old at the time, just learning to walk.

A family member came out onto the pier. He decided to have some fun with Dustin. He approached him suddenly in a mock scarey tone: "I am going to get you, Dustin!" Dustin took a step back, and fell into the water.

Most of my memories are like video tape. This one is like a still shot. I will always remember little Dustin floating face down in the water. I was completely across the pier and

> **When you think of what he has done for you, is this too much to ask?**

could not get to him. What a horrible sight to see your son floating motionless, face down in the water.

This family member, who had scared Dustin in the water, did not take off his watch. He did not take off his shoes or take his wallet out of his pocket. He jumped into the water. It was about waist deep. Quickly, he pulled Dustin out and Dustin is doing fine to this day.

Here is my question. How would you rate this act on the part of this family member? Would you say that this was in incredible act of heroism that ought to be featured in *USA Today*? Should he be interviewed on *Good Morning America* and the *Today Show*? Or was this a good thing, but the normal thing that a normal person would have done under similar circumstances? I think it was a good thing. He may have saved my son's life, and I don't want to underestimate my appreciation and gratitude. Still, I would say this is a normal thing that a normal person would have done under similar circumstances.

I think this is the kind of thought Paul had in mind when he wrote, "When you think of what he has done for you, is this too much to ask?" (Romans 12:1; NLT).

Think about it. Think about all that God has done for you. He has given you the forgiveness of sins. What would you pay for that if you had to pay for it? What would you give to have your sins forgiven? What

> **Lord, thank you for the color of the green leaves outside.**

would you do to earn the privilege of having your sins forgiven if you could earn it? In light of forgiveness, is it too much to ask that you give yourself to using your gifts to grow your groups to double your class every two years or less?

Think about the Bible. God's Word guides us, comforts us, instructs us, and convicts us. It is absolutely trustworthy and can be counted on completely. What would you pay for that? What would you give for a Bible if you did not have one? You have a Bible! Is it too much to ask that you would give yourself to the magnificent obsession of doubling a group?

I heard a brother pray recently, "Lord, thank you for the color of the green leaves outside." I found myself praying, "Lord, make my heart more observant, more tender, more grateful like his." God has given us the color green in leaves, and a million other beautiful things to enjoy. Live in grateful service.

In light of all that God has done for us, is it too much to ask that you would give yourself to the magnificent obsession of doubling your group every two years or less?

Reason #10: Because of the Reward

The Bible clearly teaches that salvation is given to us as a gift of God, not of works lest any man should boast (Ephesians 2:8-9). Salvation comes by grace through faith, but rewards come on the basis of works. Look at what the Bible says:

"For the Son of Man is going to come in his Father's glory with his angels, and then he will reward each person according to what he has done." (Matthew 16:27)

God "will give to each person according to what he has done." (Romans 2:6)

> **Salvation is given to us by grace through faith. Rewards are given on the basis of works.**

"Behold, I am coming soon! My reward is with me, and I will give to everyone according to what he has done." (Rev. 22:12)

Salvation is given to us by grace through faith. Rewards are given on the basis of works. If you aspire to be rewarded greatly in heaven (and the Lord delights in your strong desire), give yourself to the high and holy calling of using your gifts to grow your groups to double your group every two years or less.

Reason #11: Because of the Cross

I have a friend who lost her son in a hiking accident in the Organ Mountains just east of Las Cruces. Those rugged, beautiful mountains seem to claim the lives of one or two young people each year. It seems we just cannot resist the lure of getting oh -too-close to their beauty and ruggedness.

It has been years now, but every time I see her I wonder how she is doing. I wonder if she still thinks of him every day, or is it all day? I wonder if she has ever gotten over it.

We assume that people ought to get over things in time. We assume that given enough time things will return to normal, and we won't think about it any more; we won't grieve anymore; we won't cry anymore. Given enough time, we ought to get over it.

I don't think the heavenly Father has ever gotten over the cross. I know that if I gave up the life of my son to save your life, I might not ever get over it. There would never be a day when I would not think about it. I would also think you ought to think about it every day. It would be hurtful if you got over it too quickly. The cross ought to continually motivate us to serve our gracious God and seek to double our groups every two years or less.

Is there anything that would cause you to give up the life of one of your kids? I wouldn't have thought so until I went through my divorce.

Divorce has given me an understanding of the heart of God in terms of reconciliation–the purpose of the cross. There have been times I found myself thinking, "I would do anything to reconcile. I would give up any amount of money, my career, any possessions, anything. I think I would give up the life of one of my kids to reconcile." [8] In those moments when I have felt that way, I have been closest to the heart of God. Because that is exactly what he did. He gave the life of His one and only Son so he might be reconciled to us.

Never get over it. Give your life to the magnificent obsession because of the cross.

---

[8]I am describing a moment more than an ongoing feeling; I am not suggesting I would have done anything about this feeling had it been somehow possible.

Reason #12: For the Glory of God

Ultimately, it is not about me. It is not about how much fun this is to double every two years or less.

In an ultimate sense, it is not about the lost and their eternal destiny.

It is not about the sickness that is in our world.

It is not about the fantastic math of multiplication.

Ultimately, it is about God. It is all about God. Everything is about God. He is the reason for everything. Giving Him glory is the reason for everything.

Our great God deserves to be treated better than he is treated in your office and on your cul-de-sac. He deserves to be respected, trusted, admired, treasured, enjoyed, revered, and loved. He is that good. He deserves it. And because of Him, because of *Him*, we ought to give ourselves to the magnificent obsession of doubling every two years or less.